THE DORSET TEA TRAIL

A guide to the tea shops of Dorset

Jean Bella

S. B. Publical

My grateful thanks are due to George Lanning
for his advice and help and for his contribution
to the book, which includes Weymouth and
Portland tea shops and The Blue Pool, Wareham.
I would also like to thank Eric Ricketts for
his illustration of The Tea Cabin, Weymouth.

First published in 1999 by
SB Publications
c/o 19 Grove Road, Seaford, East Sussex BN25 1TP

Jean Bellamy 1999

ISBN 1 85770 182 8

Typeset by JEM Lewes
Printed by The Adland Print Group Ltd
Unit 10-11 Bellingham Trading Estate,
Franthorne Way, London SE6 3BX.
Tel: 0181-695 6262 Fax: 0181-695 6300

INTRODUCTION

TEA was discovered accidentally five thousand years ago, legend says. Apparently the Chinese Emporer Chen Nong was sitting in his garden sipping a bowl of hot water when the breeze blew some aromatic leaves into the vessel. He so enjoyed the flavour that thereafter he ordered his hot water already infused with the leaves.

In the mid-17th century tea drinking became fashionable in England. The leaves came from China on fast tea clippers, but at that time only the rich could afford to buy the tea, which they stored in locked boxes.

Those looking to make a quick profit from the costly commodity adulterated the tea with such things as dried sheeps dung or ash tree leaves soaked in copperas. John Horniman addressed the problem by setting up a business on the Isle of Wight that processed tea in sealed packets, thus preventing tampering and ensuring the correct weight.

Others, aiming to avoid the heavy taxes imposed on tea, brought it ashore illegally, packed in oil skins to keep it dry. It was not until 1784, when the tax on tea was reduced, that this smuggling activity was brought to a halt.

Interestingly, it was Richard Twining who persuaded William Pitt to reduce the tax. Twining bought a coffee shop in The Strand, London, to sell tea, and the firm is still there today, at its original address, complete with museum and shop.

As the price of tea tumbled it became the national brew — taken here, unlike in the East, with milk and sugar. Anna, Duchess of Bedford, is said to have started the tradition of afternoon tea in about 1840 by inviting friends to share dainty little sandwiches, cakes and cups of tea half way between the main midday and evening meals.

In high society tea-taking became all the rage; the ladies wore special teagowns, a new etiquette evolved and potteries started producing tea sets of matching teapot, jug, sugar bowl, cake plates and stands.

Tea rooms and tea gardens, some of them appearing to have been around for centuries, are not of such great age. They came about towards the end of the 19th century when cycling in the countryside became popular, and when the first cars were seen on the roads. Country people opened their doors to travellers cycling or motoring out from the towns, offering them a pot of tea or home made lemonade, scones, and a slice of cake. From this humble start the tea rooms we know today began.

This book is arranged alphabetically, by town or village.

Jean Bellamy 1999

ABBOTSBURY

ABBOTSBURY is situated on the spectacular scenic coastal road, the B3157, nine miles equidistant from Weymouth, Dorchester and Bridport. The historic village was built from the remains of the 12th century Benedictine Abbey of St Peter, founded 900 years ago during the reign of King Canute.

It is composed of picturesque houses and cottages of yellow-brown stone, mostly thatched, and is noted for its world-famous swannery, and for the Tropical Gardens first planted in the 18th century and open daily throughout the year. Its massive tithe barn, which originally formed part of the monastery, is now in ruins for half of its length.

On top of a steep, 250ft hill, grazed by hundreds of sheep, is St Aldhelm's Chapel, which for centuries acted as a look-out and beacon.

Abbotsbury has a variety of fascinating craft shops and galleries.

Self-Service Restaurant
Abbotsbury Sub-tropical Gardens
Beach Road
Abbotsbury
01305 871732 (Gardens: 871387)

Owner:	John Aldam
Open:	10am-5 pm daily, April to October
	(November to March dependent on weather)
Parking:	On site

The gardens, started in 1780, consist of more than twenty acres of plants and trees, set in a leafy hollow sheltered from cold winds. Many rare and exotic plants flourish and thrive in this mild climate. Peacocks roam freely, and there are lily ponds, a walled garden, a children's play area, a large plant shop and a well-stocked gift shop.

The newly opened self-service restaurant serves snacks, lunches and teas (including cream teas). All the fare is home-made, including the cakes.

The Old Schoolhouse, Gift Shop & Country Tea Room
1 Back Street
Abbotsbury
01305 871808

Owners:	Roger and Jacqui Loiselle
Open:	10.30am-5pm, closed Wednesday Two weeks off in January
Parking:	In Back Street and central car-park

Cream teas are served in this picturesque tea room, along with fresh strawberries, using Craig s local cream from Osmington. The owners specialise in home-made cakes, fruit cakes and scones, as well as local crab sandwiches served with salad and potato crisps. There is a tasty selection of light lunches, snacks, and traditional teas on the menu, the latter including Dorset apple cake in a choice of apple and toffee, apple and almond, apple and ginger.

The Old Schoolhouse was built in 1868 as the teacher s house and stood next to the village school, the latter being used as such until the early 1980s. Local crafts, cards, books and souvenirs are on sale in the gift shop.

Wheelwrights Tea Room
14 Rodden Row
Abbotsbury
81305 871800

Owners:	Sue and Nigel Melville
Open:	10.30am-5pm, Wednesday to Sunday, all year
Parking:	Free parking across the road, also in car park almost opposite (50p all day, free during winter)

Wheelwrights, on the Bridport to Weymouth Road, is a small traditional tea room in a 16th century building which attracts regular custom throughout the year. It has made its reputation on the strength of good quality tea and coffee, home-made soups, light lunches, cream and home bake teas, and cakes (all home-made), in a pleasant non-smoking environment. Ploughman s lunches, cheese rolls, quiche, and toasted tea-cakes are also available. There is a garden at the rear for *al fresco* teas and lunches in warm weather.

Until about fifty years ago, the building was a wheelwright s workshop, as it had been for four centuries. Since then it has been a glass engraver s, a potter s studio, then a baker s shop and tea room. The relaxed atmosphere is typified by classical music, candle-light, and richly embroidered hangings.

Wheelwrights is known for its exhibitions of contemporary textile work. Almost all the work on show is for sale, as are greetings cards and postcards of work by the artists. Permanently on display are a hand-dyed and hand-stitched hammock, and a half-tester canopy, the work of Sue Melville.

BEAMINSTER

THE church of St Mary, built in the early 16th century of Ham Hill stone, dominates this small and pleasant town situated where the river Brit nears it source. Houses dating from the 17th and 18th century occupy its market place and a modern market cross incorporates a war memorial.

The river flows between the Manor House in its parkland to the north, and one of Dorset's great 16th century houses to the south. Hidden in a valley, the gardens of Parnham House, with their balustraded terraces and sweeping lawns, have in recent years been enhanced by the planting of unusual trees, shrubs and borders.

In 1976 Parnham became the home of Mr and Mrs John Makepeace, in whose famous workshops craftsmen make exquisite individual pieces of furniture, designed to order.

The Oak Room Café
Parnham House and Gardens
Nr Beaminster
01308 862204

Owners:　　Mr and Mrs John Makepeace
Open:　　　10am-4.45pm, Sunday, Tuesday, Wednesday,
　　　　　　Thursday and bank holidays, April to October;
　　　　　　house, gardens and workshops, 10am-5pm
Parking:　　On site

Parnham House is a magnificent Tudor mansion that lies on the A3066, one mile south of Beaminster and five miles north of Bridport. Having visited and admired the workshops, the visitor may browse in the shop where smaller items of furniture are on sale, as well as gifts, books, postcards and colour-slides.

Afterwards, welcome refreshments are available in the attractive surroundings of the 17th century buttery, now The Oak Room Cafe. Here capuccino coffee, delicious home-made lunches and salads are served, as well as teas (including Dorset cream teas), cakes and biscuits, and a good selection of drinks. Group visits are by appointment.

8

Jenny Wren's Tea Shop
1 Hogshill Street
Beaminster
01308 862814

Owners: Debbie and Steve Paine
Open: 10.30am-5pm daily but closed Monday,
             April to October
Parking: In the square, or on-street (two hours)

Morning coffee, lunches, and cream teas are served in this 17th century tea shop with oak beams and an old fireplace.

It seats twenty and is ornamented with tea-cups of all shapes and sizes.

Articles on sale include tea towels, biscuits, dolls and cards.

Comfortable bed and breakfast accommodation is also available. Most rooms are *en suite* and one has a four-poster bed.

A day without tea is like a day without sunshine, says a calendar on the wall.

Another has this:

Thank God for tea,
Where would the world be
without tea
I am glad I was not born before tea.

And there is a third, attributed to Rudyard Kipling, which says:

We had a kettle, we let it leak
Our not repairing it made it worse,
We haven't had any tea for a week
The bottom is out of the universe.

The Tea Shoppe
6 Church Street
Beaminster
01308 862513

Owners: RV and DL Lobb
Open: Monday to Saturday, 10am-5pm; Sunday
              12-5pm; closed Tuesday
Parking: Car park in middle of square, or free
              at roadside

This little tea shop situated off The Square seats twenty, and occupies a 350-year-old building. Here you can enjoy home-made toasted snacks, including poached and scrambled eggs.

Cream teas are a speciality and include either the Dorset, West Country or Beaminster variety. All are served with straw-berry jam and clotted cream, followed by a home-made cake of your selection.

Another speciality is Moore s Dorset shortbread.

It is advisable to book in advance for the traditional Sunday lunch which includes soup of the day, roast of the day and apple pie with cream.

At The Tea Shoppe you can buy jams which come from Thursday Cottage, Carswell Farm at nearby Uplyme.

BLANDFORD

With its fine six-arched bridge over the river Stour and its Georgian town hall, this town is noted for the many fires which devastated it between 1579 and 1731. The fire of 1731 almost reduced it to a smoking ruin, following which it was rebuilt in Georgian style by Act of Parliament and public subscription.

Near the church, a Doric portico of Portland stone erected in 1760 to commemorate the event, houses a pump as a safeguard for the future. The town is also famed for its young public school, Bryanston.

The Georgian Tea Room
7 Georgian Passage
East Street
Blandford
01258 450307

Owner: Mrs C Harrison
Open: Monday and Tuesday, 9am-2pm; Wednesday to Saturday, 9am-5pm
Parking: In Market Place

It is easy to miss this tea room tucked away down a side turning off busy East Street. As you enter this interesting old building, which in its time has been, amongst other things, a wool shop and a boutique, you will notice the grape vine growing overhead. At one time there was a glove factory next door, and at another a photograhic business operated upstairs.

Lunches and Dorset cream teas are available in this non-smoking establishment (or outside under the grape vine, if fine). Everything is home-made except the bread.

11

BOURNEMOUTH

Here is a town which, like neighbouring Poole, has altered much in recent years – not for the better, some might say, remembering the genteel place Bournemouth once was.

Victorian arcades mix with modern shopping precincts, and the gigantic Bournemouth International Centre now supplements the Pavilion and Pier Theatres as a centre for top shows during the summer months. The parks and gardens, with their band concerts, flowers, shrubs and streams, remain as ever, however, and provide peace and tranquillity in the heart of this bustling town.

Cranberrys Tea Rooms
7 Criterion Arcade
Old Christchurch Road
Bournemouth
01202 315528

Owner:	Mrs Mitchell
Open:	Seven days a week, all year round, 9.30am-6pm, 10am-4pm on Sunday
Parking:	Car park, or on-street at rear

This charming restaurant and tea room is situated in the Criterion Arcade at the lower end of Old Christchurch Road. On the extensive menu are listed Dorset cream teas comprising two scones with clotted cream, local jam, cake, and a pot of tea;

Dorset apple cake served warm; a selection of local biscuits; tea-cakes, crumpets, and ice cream sundaes.

A particular epicurean experience is Cranberry's triple-decker crab sandwich, available as a special from time to time – and baked chocolate teacake is another.

There are thirteen blends of tea from which to choose, including Assam, Darjeeling, Orange Pekoe and Jasmine.

Kristy's Tea Rooms and Restaurant
33 Seamoor Road
Westbourne
Bournemouth
01202 751141

Owner: Mr Burningham
Open: Normally 9.30am-5pm, daily;
             closed bank holidays
Parking: Outside and in car park opposite

This cheerful, red-painted, fully-licensed restaurant and tea room in Westbourne has a seating capacity of around sixty, with extra accommodation in the garden when fine. Tea is taken from fine bone-china cups and saucers and only bone-china teapots are used. Bread, cakes, and preserves are all home- baked, full Cream Teas include home-made scones, jam, clotted cream, cucumber sandwiches and a choice of cakes.

Breakfasts are also available, as are snacks, jacket potatoes, salads, sandwiches and baguettes.

There is an antiques sale room at the back of the restaurant.

Muffins
8 Westbourne Arcade
Westbourne
Bournemouth
01202 757644

Owners: June Hughes and Wendy Westwood
Open: 9.30am-5pm all the year, Monday to
             Saturday, but not bank holidays
Parking: Limited on-street parking

In this licensed continental cafe in the Arcade you may enjoy cream teas, plain teas, lunches, snacks, tasty sandwiches, soups, jacket potatoes, savoury muffins topped with tomato and tuna pat , grilled cheese, or fruit pie with cream.

13

Cream teas comprise two scones (either plain, sultana, or cherry), with butter, strawberry preserve, cream, and a pot of tea.

The popular Shopper's Tea consists of a toasted and buttered crumpet served with a slice of cake and a pot of tea for one.

Bournemouth Arcade

BRIDPORT

SITUATED in a valley where the River Brit meets the Asker, this south coast Dorset town was, since the 13th century, involved in the making of fishing nets and cordage for ropes. Hence the wide streets necessary for spreading the nets, and the narrow streets (called rope-walks) leading off, which provided the required length for the handling of the ropes.

Georgian brick and stone-faced buildings line the main street, and half-way down is the Town Hall with clock tower and cupola. Nearby West Bay has a small narrow entrance harbour and is a place not greatly altered since the 19th century.

Hussey's Tea Room
38 West Street
Bridport
01308 422384

Owners:	Janet and Michael Hussey
Open:	Monday to Wednesday, and Friday, 9am-4pm, Thursday 9am-3.30pm, Saturday 8.30am-4.30pm
Parking:	In municipal car park at rear

The bakery business (Hussey s Bakers) attached to these tea rooms was established in 1911 by Mr Hussey s grandfather. It moved to the present listed building in 1938, and the tea room was opened in 1994.

Snacks, including jacket potatoes, hot sausages and quiches, are available, as well as cream teas, plain teas and Dorset apple cake. Iced buns, treacle tarts, doughnuts and lardy cake are on offer, but if you do not see the cake of your choice in the tea room, you may go next door and select one from the bakery where they are made.

The little tea room seats twenty five, and while you are enjoying your meal, you may admire the antique teapots which ornament the shelves around the walls.

Toby Jug Coffee Shop
41 South Street
Bridport
01308 422115

Owners: Roger and Veronica Hanks
Open: 9am-5pm daily except Saturday
Parking: Large park; also on-street

This fine listed building is on the western side of South Street between the cinema and the museum. It has a *c*1700 facade, but the interior has been modernised. The Toby Jug Coffee Shop seats thirty two and serves breakfasts, lunches — including steak and kidney pies and cottage pies — snacks, cream teas, Dorset apple cake and pastries, to name but a selection.

All its food is made on the premises, and you can be sure of a good meal.

16

BROADWINDSOR

IN this village seven miles north of Bridport, Charles Ii took refuge during the Civil War, when fleeing from the Parliamentary troops after the Battle of Worcester in 1651. Dressed as a lady s servant, he narrowly escaped capture in the little village inn where he was hiding. The building was burned down in 1856, but today a cottage on the site bears a plaque commemorating the event.

The Craft and Design Centre
Broadwindsor
01308 868362

Owner:	Ruth Guilor
Open:	10am-5pm daily, March 1 to December 23
Parking:	Large free car park; coaches by appointment

This is a family-owned enterprise housed in a converted farm complex on the edge of the village in the hidden valley of the River Brit. It opened in 1986 and is now home to nine independent craft businesses. Opening times of workshops and studios may differ from those of the main shop and restaurant.

The large shop sells quality gifts, and the award-winning restaurant and conservatory (seating eighty five plus) serves morning coffee, milkshakes, lunches, and afternoon teas. For lunch, homemade soups, hot dishes and salads using fresh produce are available daily.

Fine coffees, teas (including herbal), with a choice of pastries and cakes (including carrot cake) may be enjoyed mornings and afternoons. Dorset cream teas are a speciality.

BROWNSEA ISLAND

PRIVATELY owned until acquired by The National Trust in 1962, Brownsea is the larges of the islands in Poole Harbour and is an ideal destination for a day out. Tranquil and remote, it consists of 500 acres of heath and woodlands, where the visitor may wander at will, although the paths are uneven in places. In 1907 General Robert Baden Powell established his first camp for Boy Scouts here.

There is a castle on the island, built by Henry VIII to protect the harbour entrance. It was converted to a home in the 18th century.

The island has a rich variety of wildlife, including the now rare red squirrel, and many species of birds. Part of the island is leased to Dorset Wildlife Trust as a nature reserve, and tours take place daily, from 2.30pm.

Brownsea Island Cafe
Brownsea Island
01202 700244

Owner: The National Trust
Open: 10.15am-30 minutes before last boat leaves
Parking: Pottery Pier (for boat owners)

Coffee, snacks and teas are available in the cafe near the landing quay.

Boats leave from Swanage, Bournemouth, Sandbanks and Poole Quay, and visitors may land from their own boats at the west of the island.

Brownsea is open from the beginning of April to the beginning of October, 10am to 6pm daily. Events during the summer include an open-air theatre. Dogs are not allowed on the island.

BURTON BRADSTOCK

BURTON Bradstock lies sheltered in the Bride Valley, and possesses a justifiable reputation for beauty. It has won numerous county awards for Best Kept Village, and in 1998 won the national Village of The Year award.

Although considerably extended in recent years, the village's new buildings blend well with the 17th century thatched houses and terraced cottages which border a labyrinth of narrow lanes.

The village lies close to the sea, and here terminates that strange phenomenon, the Chesil Beach, which extends from Portland sixteen miles distant. The beach consists of a great bank of shingle, with stones decreasing in size the nearer they get to Burton Bradstock, many ships have been cast up onto this treacherous shore.

Bridge Cottage Stores, Tea Room & Guest Rooms
87 High Street
Burton Bradstock
01308 897222

Owner: Geoffrey and Sandra Payne

Open: Monday to Saturday, 9am-7pm; Sunday 9am-5pm, summer only

Parking: In lay-by opposite

There is a small tea room attached to this general store where fine tea and coffee is served, and clotted cream teas may be enjoyed either inside or out.

There are also *en suite* guest rooms for bed and breakfast visitors.

The Hive Cafe
Hive Beach
Burton Bradstock
01308 897070

Owner:	The National Trust
Open:	10am-6pm daily, summer; 10am-3.30pm daily, winter, weather permitting
Parking:	Car park, free in winter

This popular cafe, right on the beach front, seats eighteen inside and sixty to seventy outside.

Here you may enjoy, with a full view of the sea, breakfasts, light lunches (fish and chips, jacket potatoes, sea food soup and crab salad), and afternoon teas including clotted cream teas, scones and home-made cakes.

Hive Beach, a popular beauty spot, is owned and maintained by The National Trust.

CERNE ABBAS

THIS old and beautiful village stands on the River Cerne and was once a famous coach staging post. At the top of Abbey Street is an impressive house built around the gateway of the old Benedictine Abbey, and to the right of it is the Abbot's Porch (which may be visited) and the Abbey Guest House where Margaret of Anjou, wife of Henry VI, is said to have stayed with her son before the battle of Tewkesbury in 1471.

The Cerne Abbas Giant

For a time, after the closing of the Abbey in 1539, Cerne maintained its status as a prosperous town with such industries as shoe-making and beer-brewing. With the coming of the railway to Dorset, however, it fell into decline, although the crushing mill in Mill Lane operated until 1933.

Ancient Abbey Street is believed to have been built *c*1400 as workshops and ancillary buildings of the Abbey, and contains a range of mediaeval timbered houses from around *c*1500. Other houses and inns are of only slightly later date, and many of these are occupied and incorporate fragments of the abbey. At the lower end of the street stands St Mary's church with its 15th century tower, and ancient stocks in the churchyard. The abbey's 15th century tithe barn is at the southern end of the village.

Singing Kettle Tea Room and Garden
7 Long Street
Cerne Abbas
01300 341349

Owners:	Terry and Pat Dean
Open:	Daily except Monday (but open bank holidays), April to the end September, 10.30am-5.30pm Saturday and Sunday only during winter
Parking:	In the road outside

Bed and Breakfast with full English breakfast, morning coffees and afternoon teas are served at the Singing Kettle, a three-storey, non-smoking establishment which is Grade II-listed, and stands in the main thoroughfare of the village at the corner of Duck Street. The building is believed to date from around 1750, and it over-looks the New Inn, once the coaching stop. In 1922 it was a drapery, after which it was used as the office of the Registrar of Births, Marriages, amd Deaths. Later, a cafe was opened in the building, a usage which seems to have continued. Little of the original structure has altered except for the addition of modern facilities.

The tea room possesses an old world charm and provides seating for thirty-six. There is a tea garden at the rear which can be reached from Mill Lane, and where dogs are welcomed.

The all-day menu includes a selection of light meals such as toasted sandwiches, jacket potatoes and omelettes. Special teas supplement the selection of cakes, scones, and tea cakes, and Dorset apple cake is served warm with clotted cream or ice cream.

The Old Market House
Georgian Tea Rooms
Cerne Abbas
01300 341680

Owner:	Mr J Smith
Open:	Daily in summer except Tuesday, 10am-6pm; weekends only in winter
Parking:	In the road

This attractive building, dating from approximately 1750, occupies the site of The Shambles — a row of covered stalls and shops where goods, especially meat, were sold — and stands in a prominent position facing up the main thoroughfare.

All-fresh food is served in this attractive tea room where morning coffee, lunches, and afternoon teas are available.

CHARMOUTH

SITUATED three miles east of Lyme Regis on the A35, this coastal village is now by-passed.

'Sweet and retired' was how Jane Austin described it, as she sat 'in unwearied contemplation' and watched the tide flow in.

Here, too, Charles II had one of his narrowest escapes following his flight after the battle of Worcester.

Stow House
The Street
Charmouth
01297 560603

Owners: Maureen and Derrick Kent
Open: Daily, except Wednesday, 10.30am-5pm;
     March to end of September,
     weather permitting
Parking: Outside tea shop (one hour)

This pretty licenced tea shop dates from 1640 and is a listed building. Said to have been at one time a house of rest for the monks of Forde Abbey, it nestles in the glorious Dorset countryside and is five minutes' level walk from the sea. At one time it was just a farm.

Food is available all day, along with hot and cold drinks. Morning coffee, light lunches with local cider or a glass of wine, and afternoon teas are served in the tea room; or, if fine in the

picturesque walled garden where you can choose between the open sunny lawn, or the covered, shaded terrace.

The varied menu includes pizza with salad, tuna fish salad, and ploughman's lunches; or you may choose a traditional Dorset cream tea or freshly cut sandwiches with home-made cakes.

24

CHRISTCHURCH

ONCE belonging to Hampshire but annexed by Dorset twenty-six years ago, the little town of Christchurch, originally known as Twynham, is dominated by its magnificent Priory which has occupied the site for nearly nine centuries. It is the longest parish church in the country and receives many visitors during the year.

Also much frequented is the Convent Walk beside the Millstream. Lying in the shadow of the priory and the castle ruins, it is approached from the quayside and comes out at the town bridge which spans the River Avon.

The New Forest Perfumery, Gift Shop and Tearooms
The Old Courthouse
11 Castle Street
Christchurch
01202 482893

Owners: Bob and Heather FitzGibbon
Open: Monday to Saturday 10am-5 pm
                  (10am-4pm in winter), 11am-5pm Sunday
Parking: Car park nearby

The actual date of this lovely old building, situated next to the castle gateway, is unknown but it is thought to be more than 700 years old. The mediaeval timber-framed building has altered over the centuries; the back having been extended, and the decorative gable end added in the last century.

The back parlour, now part of the tea shop, was used as a court room for many years – hence the name. From 1827 it became a butcher's shop, traces of this occupation being still visible in the meat-hanging rails above the ground-floor windows, and the hooks in the beams in the tea room. It then became a book shop, and in 1936 the perfumery business, originally from Lyndhurst, was launched. The present owners bought it in 1988, carrying on the tradition of perfume-making. New Forest Pine Cologne, acclaimed for four generations for the relief of colds, catarrh, headaches and hayfever, may be purchased as well as perfumes in the style of many well known fragrances. In 1996 the ground floor living area was turned into old style tea rooms serving home-made food.

Ducking Stool Tea Rooms
13A Ducking Stool Lane
Milhams Street
Christchurch
01202 485779

Owner: Susan Tabor
Open: Monday to Saturday, 10am-5pm, all year
Parking: Outside (limited)

Eating is a pleasure in this 200-year-old building, once a blacksmith s shop. Here you may enjoy morning coffee, home-

made traditional fare, light lunches (including oven-baked jacket potatoes), plain teas and Dorset clotted cream teas. The little room adjoining sells jams, honey, teas and biscuits.

A board outside explains the name. The ducking stool was a form of punishment for scolds and nagging wives during the 15th to 18th centuries.

The culprit, who had been sentenced by the Court Leet, was raised and lowered into the mill- stream as often as the sentence directed, in order to cool her immoderate heat. In 1986, the Court Leet was re-established for the centennial festival to celebrate Queen Victoria s charter which confirmed the borough status of Christchurch. The ducking stool was re-made and was placed in its original position.

The Court Leet still meets once or twice a year to hold a mock court to punish wrongdoers and to beat the bounds.

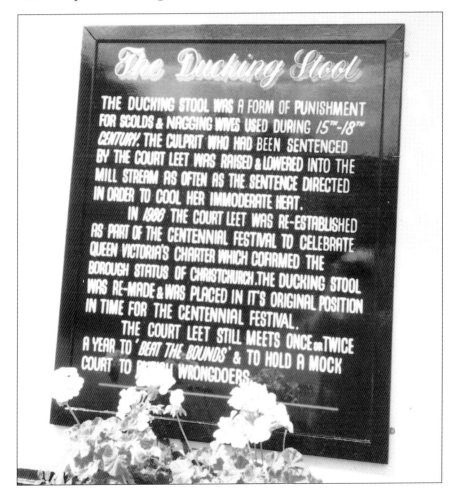

COMPTON ABBAS

SITUATED below the high curve of Melbury Hill, this village was called Cumb-Tun (a village in a narrow valley) by the Saxons. In the 13th century it became Comton Abbatisse, because of its proximity to the abbey at Shaftesbury.

Only the ivy-covered tower of the old church, destroyed in the 1860s, remains, along with a stone mounting block and the stump of an ancient preaching cross.

Coming more up to date, in the 1970s a small airfield for light aircraft and gliders came into being on the hill above, following which the villagers lost their lengthy battle to ban flying – which continued into the 1980s.

Milestones
Compton Abbas
Shaftesbury
01747 811360

Owners: R and A Smith
Open: Daily except Thursday, 10am-5.30pm,
    Sunday 10am-1pm, 2.30-5.30pm,
    Easter to November
Parking: On site, for 12 cars.

It is a delight, when travelling from Shaftesbury to Blandford, to come upon the thatched 17th century Milestone Tea Rooms in their picturesque surroundings beside the main road. Amid

beautifully laid-out gardens, lawns, trees and shrubs, you can enjoy a varied menu including light snacks, quiches, ploughman's lunches, and cheese-on-toast.

Dorset cream teas, either large or small, comprising home-made scones, jam, clotted cream, and home-made cakes, are a speciality. Or you may prefer a cottage or farmhouse tea, the latter including a new-laid boiled egg, bread-and-butter and honey.

The attractive tea room and conservatory together seat thirty, and there is additional seating out-of-doors under sunshades, when the weather is fine.

CORFE CASTLE

SITUATED four miles south of Wareham on the A351, this picturesque Purbeck stone village, dominated by the majestic ruins of its castle standing on a conical hill, is unique in the country. Here the notorious Queen Elfrida murdered (or caused to be murdered) her step-son, young King Edward, so that her own son, Ethelred, might reign instead.

Tragedy struck again during the Civil War when Lady Bankes and her servants withstood a siege of the castle by pouring hot ashes over the Parliamentary assailants. Eventually though, the castle was taken by the treachery of a member of the garrison. In 1645, Parliament ordered the castle to be blown up.

Today, however, the village is a peaceful place, well stocked with visitors during the summer months.

National Trust Tea Shop
The Square
Corfe Castle
01929 481332

Owner:	The National Trust
Open:	12-5.30pm daily
Parking:	In the road or nearby car park

Customers may enjoy three types of afternoon tea in this popular, non-smoking tea shop — Clotted Cream Tea, Gardeners Tea (comprising a pot of tea with cheese scone and butter and a slice of home-made cake), and Purbeck Tea (pot of tea with locally baked bread and butter and strawberry preserve and a slice of home-made cake). Toasted tea-cakes, and a selection of home-made cakes are also available, and much else besides, including breakfasts and lunches.

Christmas party bookings of up to fifty people are catered for too, these being particularly welcome on Thursdays and Fridays throughout December.

Marblers
5 West Street
Corfe Castle
01929 480326

Owners:	Mr and Mrs EAJ Buckhurst
Open:	Summer, 10am-5pm; winter 10am-4.30pm; closed Monday (except bank holidays and in school holidays), and closed January
Parking:	In street (not outside shop), or nearby car park

In this attractive building dating from the 1700s the visitor may

enjoy a cream tea, home-made sandwiches, home-made biscuits and home-made cakes. In the well-stocked gift shop, secondhand Poole pottery of the original — and now valuable — variety is on sale.

The name of this tea shop is a reminder of the one of the oldest and most interesting of the customs of the Isle of

31

Purbeck, one having connections with the quarrymen of the district who were known as the Purbeck marblers. On Shrove Tuesday, the Freemen of the Ancient Order of Marblers held their annual court to introduce new Freemen at the castle.

 After assembling in Corfe Castle Town Hall for the ceremony, they would play a game of street football along the Corfe to Swanage road and back again to the castle, the purpose being to maintain an ancient right-of-way to Swanage Harbour from which Purbeck marble was once shipped.

Today, on Shrove Tuesday, the custom is still observed.

CRANBORNE

LYING nineteen miles north of Wimborne on the B3078, this peaceful little place was once an important market town, with a market held every week and a fair twice a year. Cranborne is steeped in history and has a magnificent manor house, mainly Tudor, dating back to the reign of Henry VIII. Many noble and royal visitors have been entertained here, including James I when he came to hunt in nearby Cranborne Chase.

An area of rolling countryside, the Chase is crossed from east to west by a belt of woods, stretching as far as the escarpment overlooking Blackmore Vale. A garrison of troops protected the kings who hunted there.

Cranborne Church was built in 1252 on the foundations of a monastery, and at 141ft in length is one of the largest in the county.

Tea Room
Cranborne Garden Centre and Nurseries
Cranborne
01725 517248

Owner:	Run by the WI
Open:	Easter to end of September/October (dependent on weather) 10am-5pm, every day
Parking:	On site car park

This is a tea room with a difference – a small garden room in the extensive Cranborne Garden Centre and Nurseries, run by members of the local Women's Institute and volunteers. There is seating for sixty (inside and out), and home-made cakes (including delicious chocolate and coffee sponges), teas, sandwiches, and ice-cream are on offer.

There are cards, biscuits, and other small items for sale and all proceeds go to the local church and other charities.

The garden centre is open Monday to Saturday, 9am-5pm; Sunday and bank holidays, 10am-5pm (4pm in January and February).

Also worthy of mention is the stupendous tea laid on (Sunday only, 3.30-5.30pm) from Easter to September in the village hall of neighbouring **Wimborne St Giles**. *This too is run by the WI with proceeds to local charities. Trestle tables groan with delicious home-made cakes, sandwiches and much more besides.*

34

DORCHESTER

KNOWN as Durnovaria to the Romans and referred to as Casterbridge in Thomas Hardy's novels, Dorchester, the county town, has many attractions. There are, for instance, three museums. The Dinosaur Museum is a great favourite with children, the Military Museum illustrates the 200 years history of the Dorsetshire Regiment and the County Museum is acknowledged to be one of the finest archaeological museums in the country. A recent addition to the County Museum is the Writers' Gallery in which memorabilia of Dorset's most famous writers are displayed. These include Hardy's study and Barnes's lectern which he used for family prayers. A statue of William Barnes, the famous parson-poet, notable for his vernacular verse, stands outside St Peter's Church, next to the museum, and one of Hardy is situated at Top o' Town.

Other places worth visiting are the Neolithic Maumbury Rings, which have earthen banks up to thirty feet high – until 1767 the site of 'Hanging Fairs', and Maiden Castle, one of the largest earthworks in the country and the site of a fierce battle between the invading Romans and the British occupants.

Judge Jeffreys' Restaurant and Lodgings
6 High West Street
Dorchester
01305 264369

Owners:	Mr and Mrs M Burr
Open:	Monday and Tuesday 9.30am-5pm; Wednesday-Saturday 9.30am-5pm, 7pm-10pm; Sunday 12-3pm
Parking:	Nearest car-park, Top o' Town

Warm hospitality, freshly home-cooked food, courtyard gardens, open fires, exciting vegetarian dishes, and non-smoking areas are on offer at this famous restaurant steeped in history. Families are very welcome, and coach

 and private parties are catered for in three separate rooms. The history of the 600-year-old building, with its carved oak frontage and little balcony bearing the face of the notorious Judge Jeffreys, has been traced from the year 1398. The present-day restaurant is a far cry, however, from the events of 1685 when the Duke of Monmouth, natural son of Charles II, returned to England on the death of his father. Attempting to assert his right to the throne, he was defeated at the Battle of Sedgemoor and subsequently executed.

George, Lord Jeffreys, Chief Justice of the King's Bench, took up residence in the house and began his notorious trials known as the Bloody Assizes. He had been ordered by James II to show no mercy to those involved with Monmouth in the Rebellion, and sentenced to death 292 prisoners, causing seventy four of them to be executed, as well as deporting many others.

Jacobean panelled rooms exist on the first floor of the building and in the restaurant on the ground floor, and Tudor fireplaces are still in use.

The Horse with the Red Umbrella
10 High West Street
Dorchester
01305 262019

Owner: John Waring
Open: All day Monday to Friday, 8am-5pm;
    Saturday 8am-5.30pm
Parking: Nearest car park, Top o' Town

At this corner-sited establishment you may enjoy a wide variety of delicious assorted home-made cakes and Danish pastries with your morning coffee or afternoon tea.

How did this restaurant came to be so quaintly-named? About

one hundred years ago there was a small theatre at the back of the premises, and the last play to be performed there was *The Horse with the Red Umbrella.* Or so the story goes.

The Old Tea House
44 High West Street
Dorchester
01305 263719

Owners:	Jim and Jan Davie
Open:	Tuesday to Sunday, 10am-5pm
	Closed Monday except bank holidays.
Parking:	At the Top o' Town car park

This charming tea house dates from 1635, and was built as an Abbot's house. Today, the facade remains much the same, apart from the Victorian bay. It became a restaurant from 1902, before which it was a bicycle shop and, earlier, provided staff accommodation for the Georgian house next door.

A 15th century Bible cover and a 12th century manuscript found in the inglenook fireplace at the front of the tea house are now in the Dorchester Museum.

This is a non-smoking establishment where food is served all day, either in one of two delightful oak-beamed tea rooms, or in the attractive walled garden. On the menu are Dorset Cream Teas (two scones, jam, clotted cream and a pot of tea), scones with butter, buttered toasted teacakes or toasted crumpets, rolls and butter, home-made cakes, and ice-cream. A choice of sandwiches is also available, as well as home-made soup with crusty roll and butter, ploughman's lunches, Welsh or buck rarebit, jacket potatoes and, that speciality of the county, Dorset apple cake.

The Mousetrap Restaurant and Tea Room
3-4 Agra Place
South Street Passage
Dorchester
01305 269101

Owners: Pat and Dennis Burroughs
Open: 10am-5pm every day including Sunday
Parking: Old Market Car Park

The Mousetrap Tea Room, fully licensed, is hidden away behind the Dolls' House Shop next to Gould's, the department store, in the narrow passage that joins the Charles Street parking area to South Street. The 1868 building, originally two cottages, was converted to a restaurant in the early 1980s when it was known as The Cookery Nook.

The attractive, welcoming little restaurant has a warm and hospitable ambience. The menu includes traditional home-cooked main meat dishes, as well as those with a Mediterranean flavour. Sunday lunches (which include roasts) are a Mousetrap specialty. Daily specials include a range of deliciously filled jacket potatoes, and baked apples with custard. Children are well catered for, too.

The Napper's Mite
South Street
Dorchester
01305 264638

Owner: Mrs Mitchell
Open: 9am-5pm, Monday to Saturday
Parking: Old Market Car Park

The Napper's Mite, much photographed and formerly an almshouse but now a licensed restaurant, is one of few old buildings to be seen in South Street. Originally known as

Napier's Almshouses, founded by Sir Robert Napier of Middlemarsh in around 1610, this fascinating building was completed by his son, Nathaniel, in 1616. Its purpose was to give shelter, in small single rooms, to ten poor men in accordance with Sir Robert's wishes. Partially rebuilt in 1842, the single rooms remained until the building became shops in the 1950s.

The restaurant seats thirty two in the coffee room, and forty outside in the courtyard and garden. Morning coffee, lunches, and snacks are on the menu and you can enjoy such specialties as fresh crab sandwiches, hot bacon rolls, sausages sandwiches, and clotted cream teas with fat-free cakes.

The fame of Napper's has spread far and wide, and there is much of interest, including the stone mullioned windows, brick chimneys, original stone doorways, and the nail studded oak door of this ancient building. Inside, on the right of the door, is an inscription with Sir Robert's coat of arms which reads: *'Built to the honour of God Bie Sir Robert Napper, Knight'*.

The clock, which originally came from the Poor Law Institution, was retained on the west front when it was rebuilt in 1842.

The Oak Room Tea Room
5 Antelope Walk
Dorchester
01305 267713

Owners:	Mr and Mrs Thompson
Open:	9.30am-4.30pm, Monday to Saturday (craft shop 9.30am-5pm)
Parking:	In main car park

Situated above Peach's Craft and Gift Shop (entrance being through the shop), this 17th century oak-panelled room has

 now been delightfully restored as a tea room in the style of a Lyons Corner House. It is reputed to have been the Courtroom of the infamous Judge Jeffreys whose Bloody Assizes, it is said, took place here when the defeated Monmouth rebels were sentenced in 1685.

Today, untroubled by thoughts of the past, you may enjoy morning coffee and lunches, and a variety of light meals, including ploughman's, jacket potatoes, and chicken curry, throughout the day. Also, of course, traditional Dorset clotted cream teas. The tea room has an atmosphere of peace and tranquillity, with waitresses in attendence clad in Victorian style black dresses, white caps and aprons.

The shop specialises in Victoriana, collectable dolls, West Country pottery, country quilts, unusual cards and framed prints.

The Peal of Gongs
15 High West Street
Dorchester
01305 262174

Owners:	Lynne and John Coleman
Open:	10am-4.30pm Monday to
	Saturday (shop, 9.30am-5pm)
Parking:	Top o' Town car park, or in road

You could easily miss this old Georgian licensed tea room, for it is tucked away behind a large gift shop. There is seating for twenty-six downstairs and further accommodation upstairs and in the garden.

Thee tables are attractively laid out with blue

the peal of gongs

and white lace cloths, and lunches and hot snacks are served until 2.15pm.

The menu includes, for example, soup with bread and butter, gammon steaks, cauliflower and broccoli bake and salad, gammon and broccoli and hot pasties. To follow, are sticky toffee pudding and custard, and treacle or jam sponge pudding with custard. Cream teas are served and all cakes and scones are home-made.

It is intriguing to learn that this old building has a well-authenticated ghost.

The Old Coach House Restaurant
Kingston Maurward
Dorchester
01305 264738

Owners:	Kingston Maurward College
Open:	Daily, 10am-5pm, except during students' Christmas holidays
Parking:	On site

Kingston Maurward House lies east of Dorchester and occupies an Edwardian garden set in an 18th century landscape. The

gardens, which include an animal park with some rare breeds, are open to the public (mid-March to the end of October, 10am-5.30pm) and comprise thirty five acres of formal gardens containing many fine trees, a Japanese garden, a national collection of penstemons and salvias, plant houses, fruit and vegetables, and a croquet lawn. A nature trail borders a magnificent five-acre lake where kingfishers may sometimes be seen.

There is a well-stocked visitor's centre which also sells plants, gifts, cards, books, and delicious Childhay Manor ice creams.

The restaurant, which was opened in June 1997 by Lord Digby, serves breakfasts, snacks and meals, and hot and cold drinks throughout the day, also Dorset cream teas.

The Coach House Restaurant
Athelampton
near Dorchester
01305 848363

Owner: Patrick Cooke
Open: Daily (except Saturday) until the end of
              October, then Sunday from November to March
Parking: On site

This beautiful and historic manor house, mainly 15th century, lies five miles east of Dorchester on the A35, and is one of the most interesting homes in England.

It is reputed to be the site of King Ahelstan's palace, and with its glorious Grade I-listed garden, walled garden, topiary pyramids, pavilions, dovecote and surrounding courts, it still retains a mediaeval air.

Snacks, lunches and cream teas are available in the Coach House Restaurant daily (except Saturday) and on Sunday visitors may enjoy roasts, fish and vegetarian dishes with waitress service. There is a four-course *a la carte* menu, and an excellent wine list.

Athelhampton was the winner of the Historic Houses Association/Christie's Garden of the Year award in 1997.

FRAMPTON

A ROMAN villa with tessellated pavements was discovered some 200 years ago in this attractive village situated in the Frome valley between Dorchester and Maiden Newton. A park runs along one side of the main road and on the other is a line of picturesque cottages and a 500-year-old church.

For centuries Frampton belonged to an abbey in Normandy to which it was given by William the Conqueror. French monks lived on a site in the park and managed the estate. They collected the rents and were said to be unpopular with the villagers who caricatured them on the capitals of two piers of the church.

Frampton Court, built in 1704 and enlarged in the 19th century by Thomas Sheridan, son of the poet, was pulled down in the 1960s. A new house was built on the site because 'the park still invites the prospect of a house'. Close by, a balustraded late 18th century bridge spans the Frome.

The Gatehouse Parlour
Olde English Tea Rooms
Frampton
01300 320280

Owners:	Lyn Woodhall and Tony Osborne
Open:	Every day except Wednesday, weekdays 10am-5pm, Saturday and Sunday 11am-5pm
Parking:	Adjoining and in the road

A little gem of a tea room, The Gatehouse Parlour was taken over and extended a few years ago by the present proprietors who now run it with their daughters, Jenine and Nichola.

Here a warm welcome awaits you and an attractive decor. Delicious teas (indoors or out) are available, as well as morning coffee, lunches and suppers.

The family also sells pine and antiques, china, gifts and cards.

HIGHER BOCKHAMPTON

EVERY year 10,000 visitors make their way to the little brick-faced cob cottage known as Hardy's Cottage at Higher Bockhampton, two miles from Stinsford, and now owned by The National Trust.

It was here, in June 1840, that Dorset's best-known author and poet, Thomas Hardy, was born, and here he wrote his novels *Desperate Remedies, Under the Greenwood Tree, A Pair of Blue Eyes* and *Far From the Madding Crowd.*

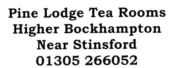

The cottage stands at the end of a deep-cut,winding, up and down lane with Yellowham Wood on one side and the heath on the other.

Hardy's heart is buried in nearby Stinsford churchyard and his ashes are in Westminster Abbey. According to a story that circulated in Dorchester at the time of his death, however, his heart was actually eaten by the surgeon's cat when it was placed in a saucer in the bedroom.

Hardy loved Stinsford and it features more often than any other place in his novels.

Pine Lodge Tea Rooms
Higher Bockhampton
Near Stinsford
01305 266052

Owners:	Jean and Tony Waterman and sons Leon and Christoper
Open:	Daily, 12-6pm, March to December
Parking:	In the grounds

Pine Lodge Tea Rooms at Pine Lodge Farm, opened in the summer of 1998. They are set in rural surroundings about one mile from Hardy's Cottage, and are accessible from it via woods and a right-of-way.

Customers may enjoy, indoors or outside, a ploughman's

lunch, a selection of sandwiches and cream teas with home-made cakes.

The tea rooms are a diversification of the farm's activities and afterwards you may wander around and see the shire horses and other animals, as well as a collection of military vehicles which Tony Waterman is in course of building up in one of the barns.

KINGSTON LACY

THIS 17th century stately home is situated in 254 acres of parkland between Wimborne and Badbury Rings on the B3082. It was designed by Sir Roger Pratt for Sir Ralph Bankes to replace his ruined family seat at Corfe Castle.

The thirteen acres of beautifully landscaped and woodland gardens were left to The National Trust by the Bankes family, along with a huge collection of paintings, Egyptian artefacts, and other works of art belonging to William Bankes.

The park, with its waymarked walks and Red Devon cattle, and the garden, restaurant and shop are all accessible.

Regular musical and other events are held during the summer, and there are special snowdrop and spring flower days.

The Stables Restaurant
Kingston Lacy
01202 883402

Owner: The National Trust
Open: 11am-6pm daily March 28 to November 1; 11am-4pm Friday, Saturday and Sunday November 2 to December 21
Parking: In car park

Morning coffee, lunch and afternoon tea are available in this licensed restaurant. Cream teas, Dorset apple cake and carrot

cake are included on the menu, and everything is home-made.

There is seating for 120 inside and 100 outside. The restaurant occupies an old stable block and horse box divisions are still in situ.

LITTON CHENEY

LITTON Cheney is a peaceful village lying eight miles west of Dorchester off the A35. Situated in a valley with a stream, it is a place to enjoy a country walk.

A 15th century church and the old rectory stand on a rise overlooking 17th and 18th century cottages and farms of local yellow stone.

Strip lynchets from Saxon times, a primitive form of agriculture, may be seen cut into the hillside to the east.

**White Cross Tea Shop
Litton Cheney
01308 482657**

Owners: Mr and Mrs LR Blair
Open: 2-5pm Tuesday to Friday, March to October
            (sometimes on Mondays and at weekends;
            also on Sundays in December)
Parking: Car park at rear, opposite youth hostel

Set teas, cream teas, lunches and snacks are available at this tea shop which is conveniently situated for walkers, hikers and cyclists. It opened in August 1998 and is already a popular stopping-off place.

There is seating for forty-five inside; outside there is a large sheltered cottage tea garden. An unusual feature on the menu (probably unique) is the full Spanish lunch, another being high tea with boiled eggs.

A small craft shop adjoins the tea room.

LYME REGIS

SITUATED on the borders of Dorset and Devon, this little sea-side town is noted for its ancient 600ft long breakwater known as The Cobb. Said to have existed since the time of Edward I, it was rebuilt more than a century ago after a great storm, and today protects the sailing boats and pleasure craft in the small harbour.

The story of how the Duke of Monmouth landed at Lyme Regis in 1685 to gain the support of the west country against his uncle, James II, is well known, as are the disasters which followed.

On a more cheerful note, the town was a favourite with Jane Austen, who used to stay in a house on the sea front, and wrote her novel *Persuasion* following these visits.

Here also, in 1811, twelve-year-old Mary Anning discovered the skull, jaw and remains of the ichthyosaurus fossil reptile which is now in the British Museum.

Country Stocks
Georgian Tea Rooms
Aveling House
53 Broad Street
Lyme Regis
01297 443568

Owners: Marilyn and Richard Fox
Open: 10am-5 pm, seven days a week
Parking: Outside on the street

These fascinating Georgian tea rooms take their name from the stocks suspended above the doorway into the inner room, and are housed in a Grade II listed building, at the back of which lies a secret garden with ponds and statues.

The atmosphere of the tea rooms is, as you will discover, evocative of earlier times, the aim of the proprietors having been to create a little of the genteel atmosphere of the Georgian period. To this end, refinements such as tea-strainers and sugar-tongs accompany your cup of tea, which you drink to the background strains of soothing classical music.

49

Coffees, teas, light lunches and Dorset cream teas are on the menu, along with such other delights as local crab sandwiches and Prince Regent's relish, the latter consisting of a thick slice of farmhouse bread and clotted cream.

Jane Austin and her sister Cassandra may well have taken tea in this building, considered to be the finest example of Georgian architecture in the town, when they visited in 1803-4.

A glimpse of the tea rooms through the well stocked shop

MILTON ABBAS

LYING seven miles south-west of Blandford off the A354, this picturesque model village is, along with the nearby abbey, one of Dorset's showpieces. Its main street is bordered by forty double, identical thatched cottages, white-walled and evenly-spaced, standing in neat gardens. They were built 200 years ago by the first Earl of Dorchester, Squire Joseph Damer, when he effaced the nearby market town of Milton Abbas because he wanted to erect a mansion for himself near the abbey.

Today, abbey and mansion (the latter now housing a public school) stand side by side in a tranquil green valley ringed by hills. Not surprisingly, Milton Abbas took the Village of the Year Award in 1998.

The Tea Clipper
Tea and Coffee House
53a The Street
Milton Abbas
Blandford Forum
01258 880223

Owners:	Pauline and Michael Northeast
Open:	10.30am-5.30pm March to October,
	Tuesday to Sunday and bank holiday Monday
Parking:	In road, unlimited

In the Tea Clipper Tea and Coffee House you may enjoy morning coffee, light lunches, and speciality Dorset cream teas with a choice of cakes. Superior teas and the finest coffees are used.

Home-made specials include soup with a roll and butter, cheese *au gratin*, turkey and vegetable curries, jacket potatoes, Cornish pasties, toasted sandwiches, ploughman's lunches, and fruit pie and clotted cream. There is seating for thirty-five inside, with additional seating outside. Reservations are advisable for large parties.

In the gift shop there are postcards, tea towels, films, trinkets and ornaments, and visitors may read about the 'unmannerly, imperious Lord' who, to protect his seclusion, destroyed the former village of Milton Abbas, banished the grammar school, and

opened sluice gates to flood out a particularly argumentative lawyer.

Holiday apartments are available on the premises.

POOLE

MUCH here has changed in the past twenty to thirty years. Poole today combines the ancient and the modern, and is scarcely recognisable as the peaceful little town it once was. Its history stretches far back in time, and Poole Quay and the old part of the town are steeped in the past.

An important port since the 13th century, Poole possesses many old buildings, including Scaplen's Court, the Guildhall, the Customs House, and the waterfront museum. Boat trips are available to Brownsea Island and around the harbour, and ferries go to Cherbourg and the Channel Islands.

A much-altered High Street nowadays links the quay with the Dolphin Centre, the latter housing shops, the library, a sports centre and the bus station.

Some things never change, however, and Poole's lovely park with its boating and freshwater lakes remains more or less as it always was.

Old Town Tea Shop
7 High Street
Poole
01202 681888

Owner:	Marylyn Dales
Open:	10am-6pm daily during the season; usually closed December and January
Parking:	On quay, or multi-storey car park at rear

Situated close to the quay, this pleasant little oak-beamed tea shop, with seating for around twenty-six, offers cream teas, the ever-popular Dorset apple cake, local farmhouse cake, home-made soups, and hot and cold snacks.

It is conveniently sited for visitors to this part of Poole where the quay and old town have a colourful nautical heritage. Nearby lie Scaplen Court Museum, the Waterfront Museum, the Guildhall, and the Customs House, all of which reveal the town's fascinating history and character.

Butterchurn Courtyard Tea Rooms
48a High Street
Poole
01202 683337

Owner: Mrs Gregory
Open: Seven days a week in season
               (but not Sunday in winter)
Parking: In nearby car parks

This interesting old building dating from the 16th century is to be found on the right of the High Street as you walk towards the quay.

Teas, Dorset cream teas, coffees, hot chocolate, snacks and jacket potatoes may be enjoyed either indoors or outside in the beautiful courtyard at the back.

Harts Tea Shop
112 High Street
Poole
01202 685419

Owner: Sue Hart
Open: Monday to Friday 8.30/9am-5.30pm;
               Saturday 8.30am-5.30pm; Sunday 10am-4.30pm

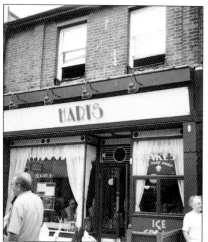

Parking: Car parks close by

As well as Dorset cream teas, toasted tea-cakes, fruit scones with butter, and Dorset apple cake, you may enjoy coffee and snacks in this attractive tea shop. Hot food on the menu includes toasted baguettes, jacket potatoes, sandwiches, tasty toasties, omelettes and Children's Specials.

Tables and chairs are set out on the pavement in front, continental style.

Poole Pottery Tea Shop and Restaurant
The Quay
Poole
01202 666200

Owner: Peter Mills
Open: Tea room 9.30am-5pm daily
Parking: Multi-storey car park nearby, and on quay

Poole Pottery is one of Dorset's most popular attractions with more than one million visitors a year. A nostalgic look back to its past takes the visitor through 2,000 years since pottery was first made in Dorset. The craft village features local crafts people demonstrating their skills in this new era of pottery production. One can even throw one's own pot, or paint one's own pottery.

Upstairs is the self-service tea room, or you may enjoy a snack from a varied menu in the Delphis Restaurant with its outstanding views; after which one can visit the clothes warehouse, and the factory shop where souvenirs are on sale, and such ranges as Dartington and Stuart Crystal at factory prices.

Poole pottery

PORTLAND

CONNECTED to the mainland by a narrow causeway, and almost an island, Portland, 496ft at its highest point, appears bleak and austere; though when the sun shines, the rugged promontory has a charm all its own.

As you ascend East Street and New Road, magnificent views open up of the famous Chesil Beach below and the countryside beyond. Four-and-a-half miles in length by one-and-three-quarters wide, this phenomenal bank of pebbles stretches 17 miles westwards towards Bridport.

Cliff-edge walks provide spectacular views, while castles, a museum, gardens, and churches give further interest. Notable at the rocky outcrop known as Portland Bill is the Pulpit Rock; also the three light-houses, one dating from 1903/6 and recently automated, another now in use as a bird observatory.

The Lobster Pot Restaurant
Portland Bill
Portland
01305 820242

Owners: Laurance Bowden and Martin Brain
Open: 10.30am-5.30pm, daily, Easter to
               end of October
Parking: Large car park nearby

This is the most southerly cafe in Dorset, situated on the cliff edge, next to the lighthouse at Portland Bill. For the visitor, it provides wonderful views of the sea and the boats as they ply to and fro.

The Lobster Pot seats seventy inside and the same number outside, and specialises in serving tea, coffee, lunches, snacks, cream teas, and fresh home-made buttered scones and cake. For the hungrier visitor there are cooked meals all day, the exten-

56

sive menu including soups, crab salad (when available), prawn salad, delicious fresh crab sandwiches, ploughman's lunch, plaice and chips, and pork sausages and chips. Peach melba, banana split and ice cream sundae are among the sweets on offer.

Delightful watercolours decorate the walls of this very popular restaurant, and there is a well-stocked gift shop as you enter.

Church Ope Cafe
223 Church Ope Road
Wakeham
Portland
01305 826179

Owner: Melanie Schofield
Open: 11am-5.30pm, summer months only
Parking: Kerbside in nearby street

This long established cafe occupies a building which is more than 100 years old, and is situated close to the Portland Museum, almost opposite Rufus Castle, on the lane leading down to Church Ope Cove. It has been under new management since October 1998.

Coffee, light lunches, snacks, sweets, cream teas and ice creams are served, as well as roasts on Sunday.

There is seating for twenty-five inside, and for the same number outside in the pleasant little garden at the side of the building.

The Yard Arm Tea Room
Portland Craft Centre
Westham
Portland
01305 823611

Owner: Timothy Jay
Open: 10am-5pm, Tuesday to Sunday (closed
                 Monday during summer; 10am-4pm winter
Parking: In the road outside

This fascinating old building close to Westham Methodist

Church contains a craft centre, a working pottery and much else to intrigue the visitor. In the gallery there is a large collection of prints and original paintings by local artists, and of particular interest is the large beam from which the tea room derives its name. This beam was the original yard arm from a ship wrecked off Portland.

In the tea room, which has seating for twenty four, the visitor may enjoy filter coffee, cream teas, home-cooked food, delicious dairy ice cream, gorgeous cakes, and a range of teas.

Bookings are taken for Sunday roasts, and visitors are invited to take their own wine.

SHAFTESBURY

THIS well-situated north Dorset Saxon town stands 700ft above sea level, overlooking the Blackmore Vale, the only hill-top town in Dorset.

A notable feature is much-photographed Gold Hill, cobbled and tremendously steep, lined with a row of attractive cottages.

There is much else here to interest the visitor, including the now enclosed ruin of the former Benedictine Abbey, preserved in a nicely laid-out site with a small museum.

The abbey is reputed to have been a gift from King Alfred the Great to his daughter who, in AD880, became the first abbess. Practically nothing remained of it following the dissolution of the monasteries.

The Salt Cellar
Licensed Restaurant and Tea Shop
Gold Hill Parade
Shaftesbury
01747 851838

Owner:	Lyn Stewart
Open:	9am-5pm, daily; closed mid-December to mid-February
Parking:	Car park in High Street

 The Salt Cellar is situated at the top of Gold Hill under the Town Hall, which dates from 1859. It has been a tea room for twelve years. From this vantage point visitors may enjoy wonderful views over the Blackmore Vale. There is seating inside for twenty, and for sixteen outside.

Morning coffee, light lunches (including soups, salads, sandwiches and vegetarian meals) are served, as well as a variety of snacks, afternoon teas and gateaux. The teas on offer include herbal, Twinings English, Earl Grey, Assam, Darjeeling and iced tea.

Everything on the menu is available for take away. There are souvenirs and picture postcards on sale.

King Alfred's Kitchen
17 High Street
Shaftesbury
Dorset
01747 852147

Owner: Mrs Newell
Open: Daily, 9.15am-5pm, Easter to October;
            11am-5pm in winter, closed Sundays
Parking: Two public car parks, or on street

This atmospheric restaurant, seating seventy, is situated in a 13th century building which has been, on and off, a tea room for centuries.

Here are served breakfasts, snacks, and lunches which include delicious home-made soups. Cream teas and plain teas are also available, along with home-made cakes.

It was intriguing, and perhaps not surprising, to learn that King Alfred's Kitchen has a ghost, which from time to time is said to cause confusion to those on the premises. Articles disappear or become misplaced, only to turn up later.

SHERBORNE

SITUATED on the northern slopes of the river Yeo valley, this town, perhaps one of the most attractive in the country, is famous for its golden-coloured abbey built of Ham Hill stone; for its ancient public school, and for its mellow mediaeval buildings including a well-preserved conduit.

Here are two castles, one built in the 12th century and given to Sir Walter Raleigh by Queen Elizabeth in 1579. He decided not to live there, however, and built the new castle in 1594 which has been in the ownership of the Digby family since 1617. The old castle has been a ruin since Cromwellian times.

Church House Gallery
Half Moon Street
Sherborne
01935 816429

Owner:	Mr NA Sargent
Open:	9am-5pm, Monday to Saturday;
	9am-4.30pm in winter
Parking:	Culverhayes car park, or on street

Morning coffee, light lunches (including soup, roll and butter, and jacket potatoes), cream teas, and take-away foods are available in this interesting oak-beamed restaurant. It is one of only a few humble Tudor town buildings to survive in the whole of England, and you can savour the air of romance which still clings to it as you enjoy a meal or morning coffee.

The building is part of the Church House built c1532-4 on land leased from the Almshouse Brethren. Originally it consisted of a large hall above, with shops and kitchen below. The walls were strengthened in 1570-1, and the date appears outside, although the stone is upside down.

The hall above was sometimes used as a theatre and it is thought possible that Sir Walter and Lady Raleigh may have been present on the occasion of the visit of the Queen's Players in 1597. In around 1700 the building was occupied by a goldsmith, a brazier, and an apothecary.

Mortimer's
5 Swanyard
Sherborne
01935 814566

Owners: Mortimer's of Yeovil
Open: 9am-5pm (Wednesday 9am-1pm);
              closed Sunday
Parking: Old Market car park nearby

'Doorsteps of toast', fresh coffee, sandwiches, rolls and light snacks are available at this little restaurant, originally a stables. Also fine teas and confectionery off the counter.

The Three Wishes Coffee Shop and Restaurant
78 Cheap Street
Sherborne
01935 817777

Owners: Jane and Tris Pinkney
Open: 9am-6pm summer; 9am-5.30pm winter
Parking: Culverhayes on right off Long Street

This wonderful old building dates from 1566, and seats fifty downstairs, and the same number upstairs. In addition there is

seating for fifty in the garden, around the attractive wishing well.

The varied menu includes breakfasts, lunches and teas, including cream teas. Specialties are Dorset apple cake, home-made apple-pie, and a more unusual item of confectionery, the Sherborne Stodger.

Last baked about 80 years ago at the Parade in Cheap Street by Mr Dewey senior, the Stodger was recently re-discovered in the book *Sherborne Camera* by Katherine Barker. It was made from enriched bun dough, with dried fruit and spice, and in those days cost sixpence for seven.

Apparently Stodgers did not last very well, so on the second day they had to be toasted, and became Gutscrapers. With the help of the restaurant's baker, Rodger Oxford (who knows Mr Dewey's son), Sherborne Stodgers are available once again – although the price has gone up a little since 1920. A pot of tea for one with a Sherborne Stodger will set you back by £2.

SHILLINGSTONE

THIS village, the name of which is derived from the Eschelling family who owned it in Norman times, winds along the main road from Sturminster Newton to Blandford for more than a mile. It is notable in the history books for the large number of volunteers who joined up on the outbreak of the First World War, thus earning for their village the title of 'England's Bravest'.

At its centre stands an ancient market cross with a richly carved modern shaft. Nearby once stood an 86ft high maypole, the tallest in Dorset.

The Willows Tea Rooms
5 Blandford Road
Shillingstone
Blandford Forum
Dorset
01258 861167

Owners:	Pat and Neil Auckland
Open:	10am-6pm daily (closed Monday) end of March to end of September; 10am-5pm October to Christmas; weekends only February and March
Parking:	Large car park nearby

You come upon The Willows, which is situated on the Blandford Road between Sturminster Newton and Blandford, somewhat unexpectedly. It is backed by fields and rolling hills, and fronted by a lawn dominated, not surprisingly, by a weeping willow. The exterior is enhanced by hanging baskets.

Inside, the lovely old tea-room has oak beams, an original inglenook fireplace and a bread oven. There is seating for twenty-six inside, and for sixteen in the garden, weather permitting.

Morning coffee, lunches and snacks are on offer, along with Dorset Apple Cake and teas with clotted cream.

On Sundays, set lunches are served between noon and 2pm, and bed and breakfast is also available.

SPETISBURY

THE name of this very long village is said to be taken from *speht* – woodpecker, and *byrig* – a fort.

It is noted for its magnificent 15th century Crawford Bridge, unusually thick and with nine arches spanning the Stour to the water-meadows, as the river winds its way south.

The earthwork known as Spetisbury Rings, seen from the other side of the river and spectacular against the skyline, is a small but strongly built Iron Age fort.

Even before the Romans arrived, it was a stronghold en route from Badbury Rings to Dorchester. Following the discovery of some eighty or ninety full-length skeletons (one skull with a four inch spear in it), Romans and Britains are thought to have been buried together side by side by the victors of some long-forgotten battle.

The church has a pulpit from Stuart times and an hourglass made in 1700.

Marigold Cottage Tea Room & Restaurant
19-20 High Street
Spetisbury
Blandford Forum
01258 452468

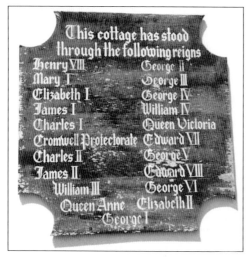

Owners: Mr and Mrs RAG Moorhouse
Open: Tuesday to Sunday, 8am-5.30pm (5pm winter); closed January
Parking: On site

Light meals are served all day in this charming old cottage dating from *c*1525, located just south-east of the church. Full of architectural interest, the listed building was, originally, two cottages and it has a large open inglenook fireplace, with two bread ovens, against the former party wall.

Hanging baskets adorn the outside walls, and a board proclaims that the cottage has stood from the reign of Henry VIII (1509-1547) through to that of George I (1714-1727); making a tally of no less than 23 reigns up to the present time.

Breakfasts, morning coffee, lunches and teas are served here. All meals are home-cooked, and cream teas and high teas are available throughout the day. The tea room is tastefully laid out with white tablecloths and blue napkins, and there are home-made cakes on sale.

There is seating for forty-four inside the cottage, and for about forty in the tea gardens.

There is a 'Sun Firemark' on the front wall, the original insurance policy register entry now being lodged with the Guildhall Library in London. It is dated 9th January 1792.

STURMINSTER NEWTON

THIS attractive market town, with its working mill, is the birth-place of Dorset's poet, William Barnes. It was also the home of Thomas Hardy for two years.

A six-arch stone bridge, built c1500, spans the River Stour and bears that amusing plaque (which may be seen on other Dorset bridges) threatening transportation for life to any person causing wilful damage to the bridge.

Poets Corner Cafe
Station Road
Sturminster Newton
Dorset.
01258 473723

Owners: Becky and Yasar
Open: 9am-5pm, Monday to Saturday,
  10am-4pm Sunday
Parking: Free car park close by

This small cafe is conveniently situated close to the town's large car park. It is run by talented cook Yasar, from Turkey, who offers exotic dishes from his homeland, including baklava, mousakka and real Turkish Delight, alongside full English and continental breakfasts and light lunches.

Cream teas are also on the menu, as well as coffee and cakes, and Yasar and Becky offer a warm welcome.

The Red Rose Restaurant and Tea Shop
Market Cross
Sturminster Newton
01258 472460

Owners: Gordon and Paul Geal
Open: 9am-5pm Monday to Saturday
Parking: Recreation ground car park

The Red Rose occupies an interesting old building dating from 1755. There is seating for fifty, inside and out. Cream teas are

available, as well as plain teas, teacakes, muffins, various delectable pastries and a wide variety of home made cakes. Teas include Assam, Darjeeling and Ceylon.

All the food is produced locally and the lunch menu includes roast beef, pork and lamb, and home made steak and kidney pie, all with fresh vegetables. There is a choice of fifteen puddings.

The owners of this interesting, old-fashioned eating house run one of the largest outside caterering businesses in the county.

SWANAGE

THE bathing is good and the sea air invigorating in this attractive seaside resort. Still much in evidence in old houses and cottages is the local grey stone.

A feature of the town is the Great Globe made from Portland stone, 10ft in diameter and weighing forty tons. On it is chiselled a map of the world surrounded by numerous quotations and strange items of information about the moon, the sun and the stars.

Another notable feature is a gothic clock tower which came from London Bridge, having been erected there as a memorial to the Duke of Wellington, and was rescued by a builder from Swanage. He also rescued the front of Mercers' Hall in Cheapside during demolition, and re-erected it as part of the Swanage Town Hall.

A picturesque corner of the town is the group of old cottages beside the Duck Pond.

Old Stable Tea Room and Gallery
37 Commercial Road (off Station Road)
Swanage
01929 424544

Owners:	EA and J Noades
Open:	10am-5pm Monday to Saturday; 10.30am-5pm Sunday May to October
Parking:	Large car park by the station

In this cosy, non-smoking, traditional tea room you may enjoy a large selection of teas, coffees, cakes (many home-made), cream teas, snacks, and home-made Dorset apple cake.

This is a small family-run business where you will be made to

70

feel welcome either downstairs or in the attractive large room upstairs, which can accommodate fifty.

Until 1947 the Victorian building was used as a stable for the local butcher's horses. The initials *W.G.W.* discovered on one of the walls are believed to stand for William Grove White, who was a local landowner.

The Harvest Kitchen
Swanage Christian Centre
36 High Street
Swanage
01929 427101

Owners:	The Churches in Swanage
Open:	9.30am-12.30pm and 2pm-5pm
	Monday to Saturday
	(early closing on Thursday)
Parking:	On street

A warm and friendly welcome awaits visitors to the Swanage Christian Centre. Here in the coffee shop set in a building dat-

ing from 1896, you may enjoy coffee, tea and light refreshments in very pleasant surroundings. There is a wide selection of Christian books, cassettes, cards and posters for sale.

The Globe, Durlston Park, Swanage.

UPWEY

THE village of Upwey lies mid-way between Weymouth and Dorchester, at the source of the five-mile River Wey.

Although still retaining the rural quality which made it a beauty spot in times past for visitors from Weymouth, it was apparently not always so. At the turn of the 19th/20th centuries it was said to be 'rather too much over-run with trippers . . . to be attractive to those who love peace and quietness when they are in the country'. In those days, a horse-drawn bus ran regular trips from Weymouth to the Wishing Well bringing visitors to wish and to enjoy strawberry cream teas under the shade of great chestnut trees.

Among Upwey's attractions are the picturesque mill beside the river and the beautiful 13th century church of St Laurence. At the opposite end of the village lies Ridgeway hill and the Old Ship Inn. For day-trippers of times past there was the added facility of the 'Upwey Wishing Well Halte' (no longer existing), conveniently placed for a 20 minute walk across fields to the Well.

It achieved fame when George III came here from Weymouth

Well-dressing at Upwey Wishing Well

73

during his frequent visits to the town to obtain relaxation from his severe mental illness. He drank the waters from a gold cup which, it is believed, became the original Ascot Gold Cup.

Upwey Wishing Well and Water Garden
161 Church Street
Upwey
Weymouth
01305 814470/812262

Owners: Mr and Mrs JR de W Harrison
Open: 10.30am-6pm daily, Easter to   end of
                September; 10.30am-5pm Wednesday to
                Sunday October 1 to December 13
Parking: On street

Considerably extended in recent years, and rebuilt following flooding in the village in January 1994, this tea room has a unique and peaceful setting overlooking a water garden. On a hot summer's day, cool shade and running water make eating outside a delight. Traditional Sunday lunches, morning coffee, delicious home cooked meals and cream teas are served and included on the menu are ploughman's lunches, hot snacks and Dorset apple cake.

In times past visitors handed over a few coins, took a glass of spring water and made a wish. Today, you can step out into the

water gardens and view the well free of charge. The water gardens are part of the National Gardens Scheme.

In the first week of May visitors are able to enjoy the added attraction of well dressing.

There is a gift shop well-stocked with chinaware, tea towels, ornaments, chocolates and local books.

WAREHAM

BUILT by the Saxons on high ground between the rivers Frome and Trent, Wareham still retains its earthern walls to the north, east and west. The layout of the little town, with streets intersecting at right angles, the four main ones dividing it into quarters, reminds visitors of its Roman past.

At the north entrance to the town is the tiny church of St Martin-on-the-Wall, believed to have been founded by St Aldhelm in 698. It contains the striking stone effigy of TE Lawrence lying full length, in flowing Arabic dress, his head resting on a camel saddle.

In Lady St Mary Church a tablet states that John Hutchins, the Dorset historian, lies buried there.

Bearly Tea Time
32 South Street
Wareham
01929 554899

Owner: Chris Simmons
Open: 10am-5.30pm, Monday to Saturday; 1-5pm Sunday
Parking: In car park opposite on quay

Superb food is on the menu in this oak-beamed, late 16th/early 17th century building where visitors can enjoy breakfasts, light lunches, cream teas, high teas, and sandwiches. The cakes are all home-made and the bread is warm and crispy.

A feature of this pretty tea shop is its display of teddy bears, to which the owner is very partial – hence its name. As well as the manufactured ones, many of the bears are hand-made and are for sale.

Originally a pub, the building was at one time larger than it is today, as it included the next-door building, now an antiques shop.

Nellie Crumb
17 South Street
Wareham
01929 552524

Owners: D and J Blackmore
Open: 9am-5.30/6pm daily in summer
               10am-4.30pm (six days only in winter)
Parking: In nearby car park on quay

Teas and cream teas are available, as well as morning snacks and lunches in this interesting Grade I-Listed building.

Looking up through the wide chimney in the tea-room, it is possible to see, below the tiled roof, the original thatch remaining from the fire of 1762 which destroyed two-thirds of the town.

The Blue Pool Tea House,
Furzebrook
Near Wareham
01929 551408

Owners:	The Furzebrook Estate
Open:	Easter to October 9.30am-5.45pm
Parking:	On site, free

Situated just south of Wareham, sign-posted off the A351 road to Swanage, the Blue Pool is one of Dorset's favourite beauty spots. The pool was once a claypit. Now it is filled with water which contains minute light-diffracting particles of clay which cause the surface colour to change intermittently from deep turquoise to emerald green. The pool is set in the midst of twenty-five acres of heather, gorse and pine trees, through which visitors may stroll before visiting the Tea House. There are some facilities for the diasabled. Dogs on leads are welcome.

The Tea House, which is close to the museum, the gift shop and the plant centre, offers morning coffee or cream teas and a mouth-watering aroma of bread, scones and cakes being baked on the premises. There is spacious seating, both indoors and on the large terrace. In 1998 The Blue Pool received the Loo of The Year award.

The museum traces the fortunes of the Furzebrook Estate, through the development of the local ball clay industry from the early 17th century when the clay was used for making tobacco pipes, until the end of the 18th century; by which time many famous pottery manufacturers had discovered the excellent white-firing properties of the clay.

WEYMOUTH

THIS well-known south coast resort, with its sweep of Georgian buildings along the seafront and a spectacular bay, has something for everyone, including safe bathing and traditional attractions.

Take a walk over the town bridge to discover the Time Walk at Brewers Quay, or visit Lodmoor Country Park, a fifteen-minute stroll from the town centre in the opposite direction.

The 17th century harbour, with its fishing and pleasure boats and yachts, is steeped in history, and the Nothe Fort and Gardens are well worth a visit.

On the hillside, George III is depicted on his great White Horse, and his statue on the promenade is impressive, as is that of Queen Victoria at the Greenhill end of the town.

Bumbles Tea and Coffee Lounge
6 Coburg Place
Weymouth
01305 786001

Owner: Mrs J Bishop
Open: Daily (except Sunday during winter)
              9am-5pm
Parking: 300 yards away, behind the public library

Being a popular seaside resort, Weymouth is full of places to eat and drink. Most of these, however, are restaurants, cafes or pubs; there are very few tea rooms. Bumbles is at the north end of St Thomas Street, one of Weymouth's two main shopping streets. It was built at the beginning of the 18th centur y and is easily recognised by its Georgian bow window on the first floor.

In the morning many customers prefer to drink coffee with their scones or cakes. During the afternoon, however, the place reverts to a typical, traditional tea room using loose tea, not tea bags. Needless to say, Dorset cream teas are very popular. So is the integrated shop where customers can buy cakes and loaves to take home. These are made at the local Sgt Bun's Bakery.

There are no car parks close to the shops in Weymouth. The nearest one to Bumbles is behind the public library some 300 yards away. An alternative is to park behind the Pavilion Theatre, about half-a-mile away, and then stroll back along the Esplanade to the beginning of St Thomas Street.

Cactus Tea Rooms
The Pleasure Pier
Weymouth
01305 781255

Owner:	Sandy Hawkins
Open:	11am-5pm, Whitsun to end of September; weekends only Easter to Whitsun
Parking:	Behind Pavilion Theatre

These tea rooms are at the end of the pier and consequently have the best views of shipping and boating activity in the bay and the estuary. To the north there is a clear view of the coast-line to the White Nothe and the hills above Lulworth Cove, and

to the south the Nothe Fort and Portland beyond.

The exterior of the rooms is rather drab, but inside they are light and attractive with a very friendly and cheery atmosphere. There is seating for forty inside, and fifty six on the sun terrace.

The menu consists of home-made cakes, speciality ice-creams, toasted sandwiches and teacakes, jacket potatoes, salads and delicious cream teas.

The owner is a big fan of Paul Young and her original intention was to call her tea rooms Los Pacaminos, which is the name of his band. Eventually, however, she chose instead to name them after the symbol of Los Pacaminos, which is a cactus.

The Tea Cabin
The Esplanade
Weymouth
01305 770770

Owners:	RD and SJ Gutteridge
Open:	Variable, according to season and weather; in summer, often 6.30am-11pm
Parking:	Car park behind Pavilion Theatre

This cafe, as its name suggests, is not so much a tea room, more a wooden cabin, yet it probably sells more cups of tea in a day than any other establishment in the town.

It has no seats inside but is licensed to have eight tables and thirty chairs outside. The cabin is on the Esplanade, next to the Tourist Information Office, and is popular with people coming off the beach. It is alongside the long-distance coach stop and is well-used by coach drivers, a fact which recalls its origins.

It was built in 1870 as a weighbridge where goods being brought ashore were weighed.

Close by, a rank of cabs formed. At some time, the proprietors of the weighbridge began to serve refreshments to the cabbies. As the use of the weighbridge declined, so the popularity for the supply of cabbies' tea increased until eventually it became simply a tea cabin.

The menu caters for everything a visitor may want -- Cornish ice-creams, hot snacks, coffee and cakes and pots of tea.

Carriages Victorian Tea Room
61b St. Thomas Street
Weymouth
01305 785511

Owner: Carina Robinson
Open: 8am-9pm daily in summer;
               8am-4.30pm daily in winter
Parking: Multi-storey car park around the corner

This tea room is at the southern end of St Thomas Street, midway between the Post Office and the bridge over the River Wey.

It opened in May, 1996, and the owner has created a Victorian theme. Waitresses wear pinnies, the tables are covered with lace cloths and many of the cakes are made from Victorian recipes.

When she was thinking of a name for the place the owner was given a photograph of St Thomas Street during Victorian times which showed a carriage passing the building. Hence the name, Carriages.

The day begins with breakfasts, followed by morning coffee, then light lunches and finally afternoon teas. All the food is cooked on the premises. Cream teas are very popular but so too are teacakes and Danish pastries.

The Lily Ponds Tearoom
Bennetts Water Gardens
Putton Lane
Chickerell
Weymouth
01305 785150

Owners: The Bennett family
Open: 10am-5pm, Tuesday to Sunday, April to August; Tuesday to Saturday, September; Tuesday to Friday, October, and bank holidays
Parking: On site

Bennetts Water Gardens are two miles west of Weymouth off the B3157 to Bridport. Here you will find the National Collection of Water Lilies in an aquatic garden centre. The project was started by Norman Bennett in 1959 in disused clay pits, formerly the Chickerell Brickworks. His success grew and soon he was exporting water lilies world-wide.

In the museum you can learn some of the history of the brickworks which supplied Weymouth and the surrounding areas in the early part of the 20th century.

The eight-acre site with its numerous lakes teeming with wildlife is still managed by the Bennett family. It has been landscaped to create a tranquil and relaxing setting where visitors may walk or sit and unwind in a scenic setting. More than 100 varieties of water lily bloom throughout the summer, and herons, kingfishers, wildfowl, and dragonflies abound.

In The Lily Ponds tea room you may enjoy morning coffee, a light lunch, home-made cakes baked on the premises or the ever popular Dorset cream tea. There is a gift shop too, and wheelchair access and disabled facilities are available.

WIMBORNE MINSTER

SET amid water meadows where the River Allen meets the Stour, the little market town of Wimborne is dominated by its squat, two-towered, ancient minster of St Cuthberga. At least two types of stone give the building a curiously mottled appearance, and inside there is a mixture of styles including Norman.

Also inside is the Orrery, or astronomical clock, dating from around 1320 and, attached to it, on the outer side of the western tower, is the famous Quarter Jack. Once a monk, but now a brightly-coloured British Grenadier, he strikes the quarter hours and has always been a great attraction, particularly for the children. In the centre of the town is the Priest's House Museum, occupying a 16th century building, and worth a visit.

The Cloisters
40 East Street
Wimborne
01202 880593

Owners: Pat and David Thomas
Open: 9am-2pm Monday to Saturday;
              10am-2pm Sunday; open all year
              except four days at Christmas
Parking: Car park nearby

These tea rooms serve very popular all day breakfasts, as well as lunches and cream teas. They are famous for their large teacakes. There is seating for sixty-two indoors, plus another ten outside in the summer. Approximately 350 plates and pictures adorn the walls, as well as artists' pictures which are for sale.

The Laughing Pot Tea Room
4 West Borough
Wimborne
01202 840676

Owners: Clive and Sandra Henry
Open: 9.30am-4.30pm Monday to Saturday all year
Parking: Car park opposite

84

The theme of this little Grade II-listed and beamed building is, not surprisingly, teapots. The owners, who have developed the shop since they took over in 1997, collect teapots of all types, shapes and colours, many of which ornament the walls.

Items on the menu include toasted sandwich specials, jacket potatoes and cream teas. All the cakes are home-baked, and there is a specialist board each day.

There are interesting items on sale in the tea shop such as bonnets, dried flower arrangements, and pictures by local artists.

The Yew Tree
7 Cook Row
Wimborne
Dorset
01202 883527

Owners:	Nigel and Rachelle
Open:	9.30am-5pm, Monday to Saturday; evening meals from 7pm Wednesday to Saturday; 11am-4pm Sunday, lunch noon-2.30pm (booking advisable)
Parking:	In The Square, or car park in West Street

This 16th century reataurant, one of Wimborne's oldest, is delightfully situated opposite the Minster church. The building has always been connected with food, and was at one time a sweet shop.

During the day the visitor may enjoy a traditional English breakfast, morning coffee, lunch, or afternoon tea served with the owners' own range of home-made cakes and scones.

A typical Sunday lunch comprises a choise of roasts as well as the usual menu; or a three-course set lunch.

The Yew Tree also offers a selection of home cooked evening meals (Wednesday to Saturday) served with local wine.

Pamphill Parlour
Pamphill
Wimborne
01202 880618

Owners:	Pamphill Dairy Farm Shop
Open:	10am-5.30pm daily
Parking:	On site

Just a mile out of Wimborne lies the peaceful hamlet of Pamphill with its thatched cottages, a village green, cricket pitch, and the little church of Kingston Lacy.

Here, in an attractively converted dairy and milking parlour, is the Pamphill Dairy Farm Shop where you may buy new-laid eggs, fresh cream, farmhouse butter, country cheeses and much else besides.

In the rural atmosphere of the Pamphill Parlour you can relax and enjoy morning coffee with home-baked cakes and pastries; luncheons comprising soups, paté, home-made pies, quiches and delicious country desserts.

Afternoon teas include home-made scones and clotted cream, tea and cakes.

When the sun shines, visitors can sit outside on the patio and enjoy the country views, while for the youngsters there is a rustic playground with climbing frame, swing and see-saw.

Local wines, ciders, pet foods, horse feeds and bales shavings are also available here.

86

WOOL

TWO miles south of Bovington Camp (the Royal Armoured Corps Centre, with its world famous Tank Museum), and a few miles to the north of Lulworth Cove is Wool, encompassed by Thomas Hardy's Great Heath.

Here a 15th century bridge over the Frome is one of the finest in the county, and next to it is one of Dorset's loveliest small manor houses, the 17th century Woolbridge Manor (scene of Tess of the D'Urberville's tragic honeymoon).

Close by are the ruins of Bindon Abbey, and on the sombre heath, Gallows Hill is one of the finest viewpoints.

Rose Mullion Restaurant and Tea Room
Wool
01929 462542

Owners:	Mrs Preen and Mrs Atwell
Open:	10am-5pm Tuesday to Sunday; two evenings a week from 7pm, May to September; 1am-4pm in winter; closed January
Parking:	Outside in road

This very attractive little licensed restaurant and tea room is almost opposite Wool Station in a 100-year-old building that has been a tea shop for twenty five years.

An extensive menu is on offer, and all the food is home-cooked and very traditional. Breakfasts, morning coffees, and teas (including Dorset clotted cream teas) and Dorset apple cake are on offer, and hot meals are available all day. There is seating inside and out for forty-three.

Candlelit suppers are a feature, and theme evenings take place during the winter.

WORTH MATRAVERS

A PROMINENT feature of this lovely stone-built village is the centrally situated duck pond. You may take a walk down through the valley to the sea, where at Winspit the surrounding hills are honeycombed with quarries.

In the churchyard lies Benjamin Jesty, whose inscription states that he was the first known person to have introduced the 'Cow Pox' by inoculation, and who from his great strength of mind, made the experiment from the cow on his wife and two sons in the year 1774. Nothing is said about the strength of mind of his wife and sons, however, who were experimented upon with a knitting needle.

Worth Teashop by the Village Green
Worth Matravers
01929 439360

Owners:	Brian and Iris Waller
Open:	10am-5.30pm seven days a week, except Tuesday in winter
Parking:	Along the road by the duck pond

At this popular tea shop (and B&B) in the Purbecks you may enjoy Dorset clotted cream teas and home-made cakes and scones, either indoors or outside in the delightful little garden at the back. Morning coffee and light lunches are on the menu, and there are local crafts and fossils on display in the shop.

DORSET APPLE CAKE

MOST of the tea shops featured in this book serve the county's speciality, Dorset apple cake, the recipe of which is well known to all true Dorset people. Some add an additional ingredient or two, according to individual tastes, some serve the cake with cream or ice cream, or hot with a caramel or toffee sauce.

For those from outside the county who may wonder what Dorset apple cake is, and who would like to try it at home, here is the basic recipe.

225g butter
4 large eggs
25g cornflour
225g chopped bramley apples
225g caster sugar
250g self-raising flour
extra apple slices
lemon juice
soft brown sugar

8oz butter

three-quarters oz cornflour
8oz chopped bramley apples
8oz caster sugar
8floz self-raising flour

Cream the butter and caster sugar together in a bowl. Add the eggs, flour and cornflour, and mix well. Fold the apples into the mixture and pour into a well -greased cake tin (18cm or 7in diameter). To decorate the cake, cut unpeeled slices of apple and soak in lemon juice, then arrange in a circular pattern on top of the cake and dust with soft brown sugar to make a crusty glaze.Bake in the oven at 170°C for about 75 minutes.

YOUR FAVOURITE TEA SHOPS

I hope you have enjoyed this little book. I apologise if I have missed out your favourite tea shop and would welcome a letter via the publisher to let me know about it.

Use this space to note details of other interesting tea rooms and cafes in Dorset, both as a personal reminder and for possible inclusion in the next edition of The Dorset Tea Trail.

Jean Bellamy

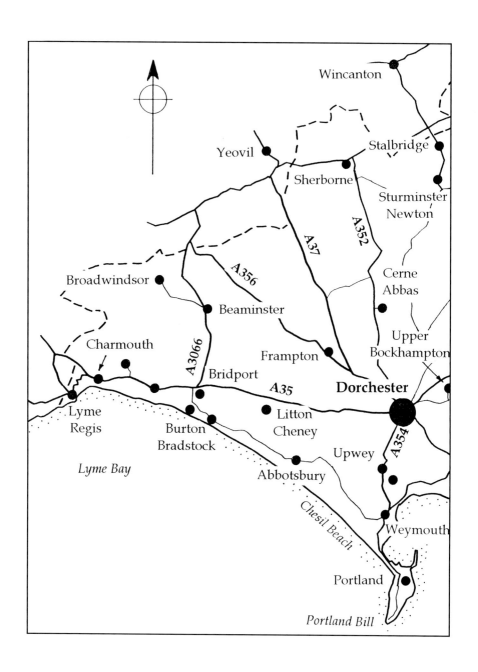

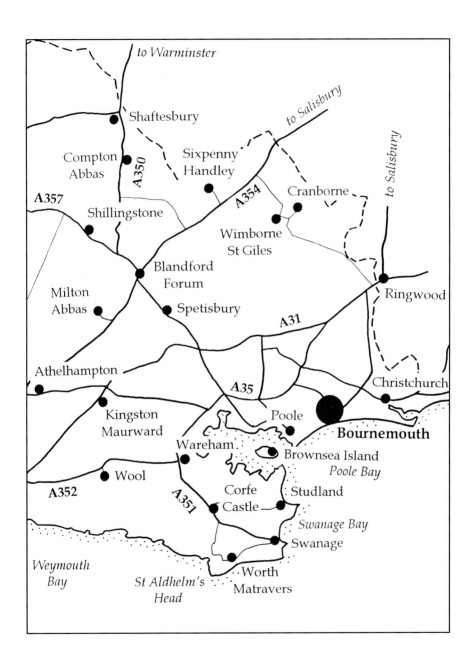

INDEX

THE AUTHOR

Jean Bellamy started her writing career in 1970 with a magazine article, shortly followed by the publication of many more articles and short stories in a wide variety of magazines, including a regular slot in *Dorset Life* magazine for nine years. Her first children's novel was published in 1986 and then followed by 2 more children's novels all with a West Country setting.

Her local history books include 'Treasures of Dorset' (1991), 'A Dorset Quiz Book' (1995) and 'A Second Dorset Quiz Book' (1997).

S. B. Publications publish a wide range of local interest books. For a full list write to:- S.B.Publications,
19 Grove Road,
Seaford,
East Sussex,
BN25 1TP.

Books on Dorset:- *A Second Dorset Quiz Book* by Jean Bellamy
Pocket Dorchester by Chris Shaw
Escape into Dorset by Chris Shaw

Front Cover:- Top left-Old Market House, Cerne Abbas.
Top right-Old Court House, Christchurch.
Bottom left-National Trust Tea Shop, Corfe Castle.
Bottom right-Tea Clipper, Milton Abbas.

Back Cover:- Marigold Cottage Tea Rooms, Spettisbury.